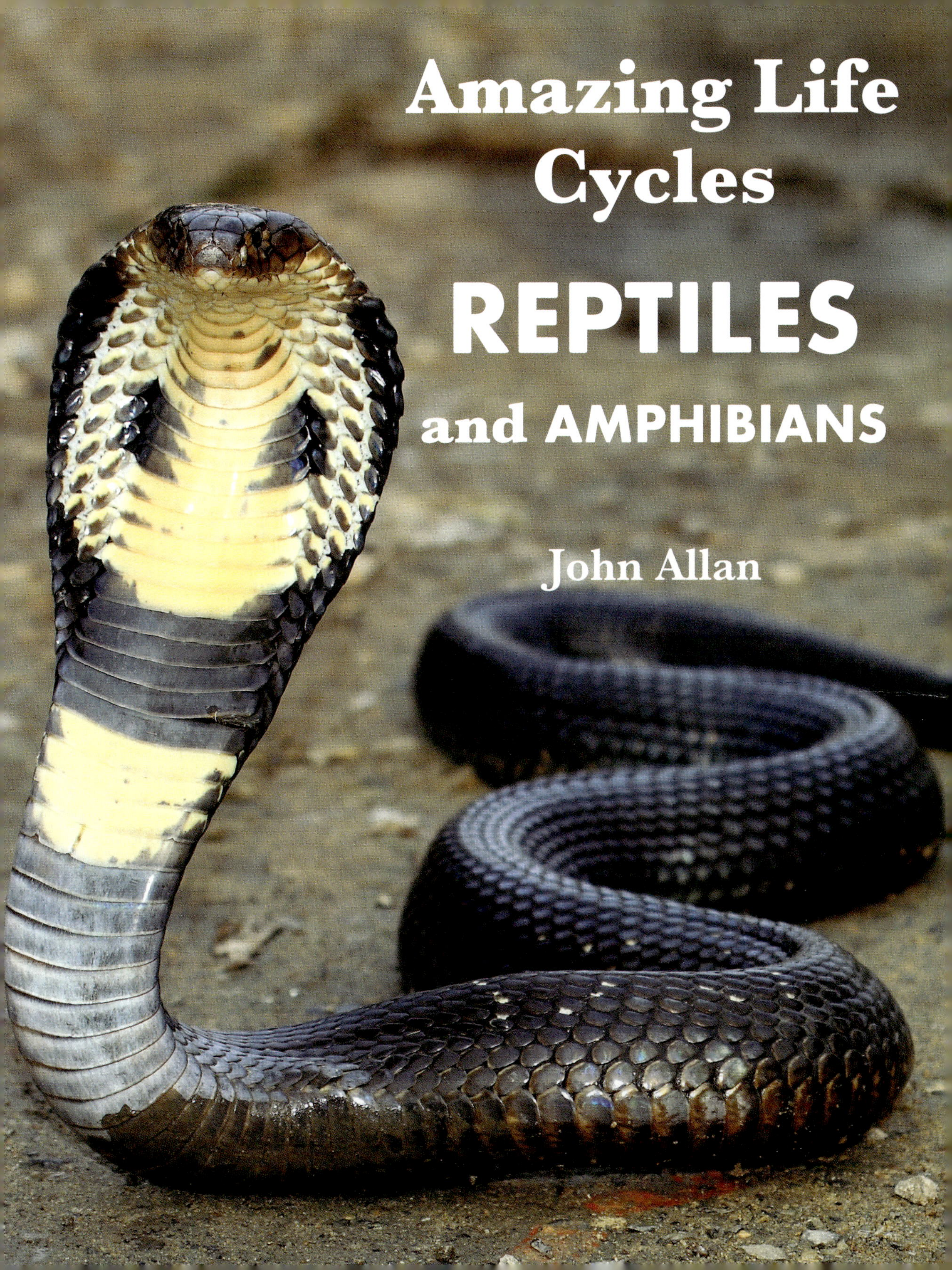

Amazing Life Cycles

REPTILES and AMPHIBIANS

John Allan

This is the endangered Hawaiian green sea turtle, which can live up to 80 years.

Contents

Words that look **bold like this** are in the glossary.

ISBN 978 1 912108 039

First published in Great Britain in 2019 by
Hungry Tomato Ltd, The Old Bakery Studios, Blewetts Wharf,
Malpas Road, Truro, Cornwall, TR1 1QH, UK

Manufactured in the United States of America

What is a reptile?

This is a crocodile's foot—you can see its scaly skin.

A reptile is an animal with a thick skin covered in scales. Reptiles are ectothermic. This means that their body temperature goes up or down with the temperature of the air or water around them.

Snakes are reptiles with no legs.

Old skin

Scales

Every few months, a snake wriggles out of its old skin. A shiny, new skin one size bigger, has grown underneath.

This lizard is growing a new tail

Lizards are reptiles. Most lizards have four legs and a tail.

If a **predator**, such as a bird, grabs a lizard's tail, the tip breaks off. The bird is left with the twitching tail. The lizard runs away and soon grows a new tail!

AMAZING REPTILE FACT

Giant Galapagos tortoises can live to be over 100 years old!

Snakes, lizards, crocodiles, alligators, tortoises and turtles are all reptiles.

Tortoises and turtles are reptiles with shells.

A giant Galapagos tortoise

This emerald tree boa gives birth to live babies.

Reptile life

Adult reptiles usually live on their own. Males and females get together to mate and then separate again. After mating most female reptiles lay eggs, but some reptiles give birth to live babies.

Most reptile mums leave their eggs to hatch on their own, but some reptiles look after their eggs.

Reptiles lay lots of eggs in one go. Only a few **hatch** – the rest are often eaten by other animals.

A female Albino darwin carpet python guards her eggs as they start to hatch

When a baby reptile hatches it looks like a tiny copy of its parents. The baby is ready to find its own food right away. Baby snakes can hunt as soon as they are born.

This small turtle has just hatched.

Male

Female

AMAZING REPTILE FACT

Reptile eggs feel rubbery. The shell is softer than a bird's egg but strong.

Chameleons are tree lizards that can change their skin color! The female shows the male she is ready to mate by changing color.

What is an amphibian?

An amphibian is an animal that lives in water and on land. Like reptiles, amphibians are ectothermic. Their bodies are the same temperature as the air or water around them. Amphibians have smooth skins.

This is a toad. It looks like a frog, but has drier, bumpier skin.

Frogs, toads, newts, salamanders and caecilians are all amphibians.

This is a caecilian. It has no legs, and looks like a snake.

Newts and salamanders are amphibians with tails.

This is a fire salamander.

The bright blue color of this poison arrow frog tells predators, "Stay away – I'm poisonous".

Frogs and toads are amphibians with no tails.

Most amphibians like warm, damp places with plenty of plants they can use as hiding places.

AMAZING AMPHIBIAN FACT

The word amphibian means "two lives"—one on land and one on water.

Amphibian eggs have no shells. A frog's eggs look like jelly.

Amphibian life

Adult amphibians usually live on their own. Males and females get together to mate. After mating, female amphibians lay eggs. Most amphibians lay their eggs in water. This stops the eggs from drying out.

In the spring, male and female frogs and toads go to ponds to mate.

Most amphibians don't look after their eggs or babies, but there are some amazing amphibian parents.

AMAZING AMPHIBIAN FACT

Male frogs puff out their throats to sing a croaky song. This attracts females.

Baby amphibians hatch from eggs. They have large heads, long tails, and breathe through **gills**, like fish. Soon they grow legs and begin breathing with lungs. Then they can live on land.

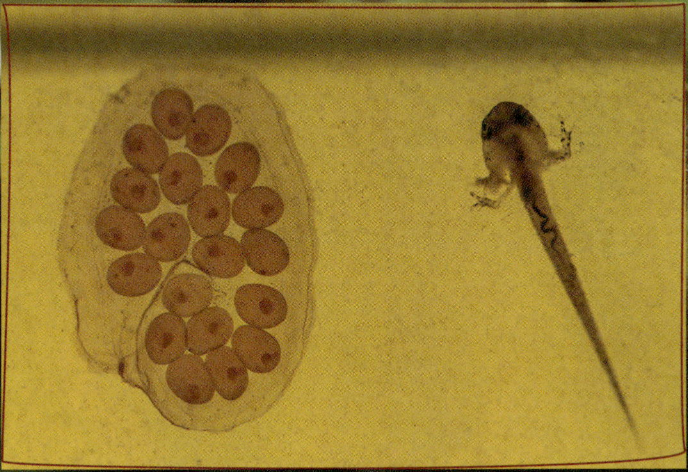

These are the young of a spotted salamander.

Some poison arrow frogs lay their eggs in water-filled hollows in trees. They carry the tadpoles to a new home if the water dries out.

Animal habitats

The sea is a habitat. Turtles live in the sea.

A habitat is the place where a plant or an animal lives. Reptiles and amphibians live in habitats from warm, wet rainforests to dry grasslands. Many amphibians live in ponds and rivers in wetlands.

Reptiles and amphibians live in all habitats except the Arctic and Antarctica.

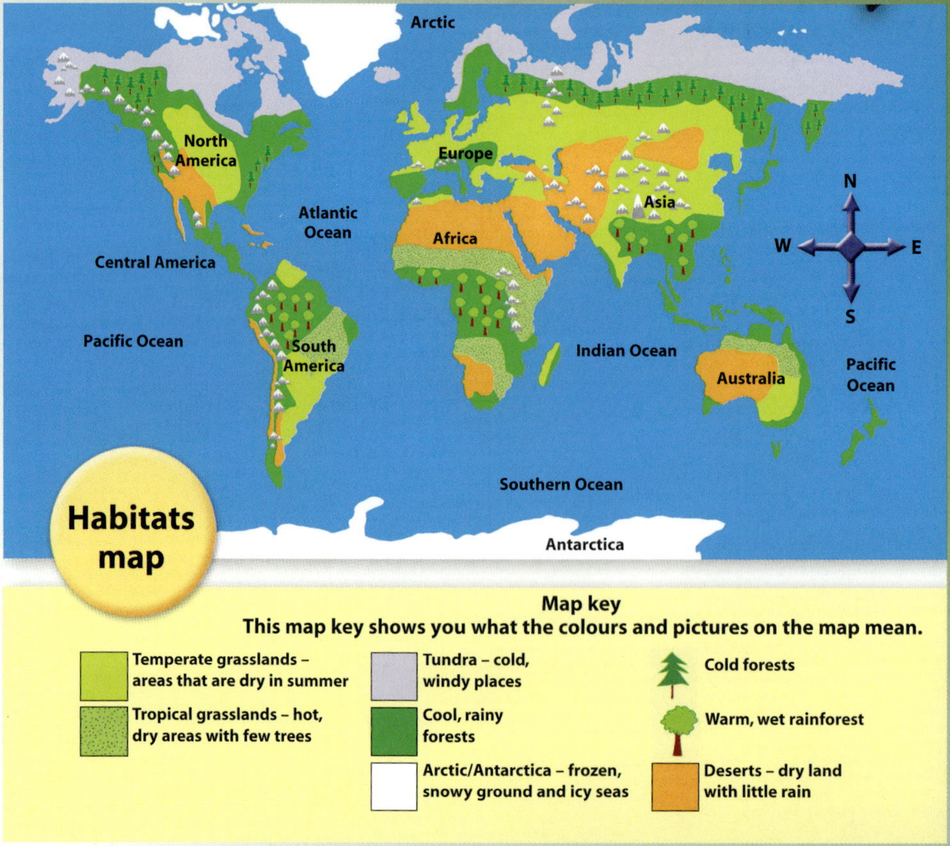

Habitats map

This thorny devil lizard lives in deserts in Australia.

Many snakes and lizards live in **deserts** which can be cold at night. In the morning, they lie in the sun to warm up their bodies.

AMAZING REPTILE FACT

There are over 1000 different kinds of tree frog.

Tree frogs live in forest habitats. This tree frog's green skin is good **camouflage** in the leaves. Its color hides it from predators and the insects it hunts.

Marine iguanas live on beaches. Large, adult marine iguanas go diving in the ocean to find seaweed to eat.

What is a life cycle?

This male Jackson's chameleon uses his horns to fight other males for females.

A life cycle is all the different stages and changes that a plant or animal goes through in its life. The diagrams on these pages show some examples of reptile and amphibian life cycles.

SNAKE LIFE CYCLE

All reptiles have a life cycle with these stages.

1

A pair of rat snakes

A male and female snake meet and mate.

2 **A Royal Python snake**

The female lays eggs. Some snakes give birth to live babies.

3 **A baby python**

Baby snakes hatch from the eggs.

4 **A young Siamese cobra**

Baby snakes are ready to go off on their own as soon as they hatch or are born.

FROG LIFE CYCLE

Most amphibianshave a life cycle with these stages.

1 An adult male and a female frog meet and mate.

2 The female lays hundreds of eggs in water.

3 Tadpoles with tails hatch from the eggs. They swim in the water and breathe through gills, like fish.

4 Over several weeks the tadpoles grow legs and lungs for breathing air on land. They lose their tails.

5 The baby frogs leave the water. They grow bigger and bigger.

Banded sea snake

Banded sea snakes live in the South Pacific

Unlike other sea snakes that complete their entire life cycle in the ocean, the banded sea snake spends an equal amount of time on land and in the sea. Courtship and mating takes place on small remote islands.

Sea snakes have long slender bodies which make them the perfect size for foraging among the reef and corals for their prey.

They survive on a diet of mainly eels and some small fish. But they also make a great meal for octopuses!

The end of their tails are flattened to give them a paddle-like effect which they use for swimming.

AMAZING REPTILE FACT
A female banded sea snake lays up to 10 eggs at a time.

They have powerful venom that will paralyze their prey and then swallow it whole. Their venom is 10 times more powerful than a rattle snake.

AMAZING REPTILE LIFE CYCLE

Nile crocodile

Nile crocodiles live beside lakes and rivers in Africa. They wait for big animals, such as antelopes, to come for a drink, then they grab them and eat them! Nile crocodiles also eat monkeys, turtles, birds and fish.

A crocodile can bite but it cannot chew.

The baby crocodiles call to their mom to let her know they are hatching.

After about 60 days the eggs hatch.

Crocodiles are fierce, but they are very good moms. They guard their eggs and even help break open the eggs with their mouths so the babies can get out.

After she has mated, the female crocodile makes a nest beside the river. She lays between 50 and 60 eggs.

AMAZING REPTILE FACT
A male Nile crocodile can grow to 19.7 ft (6 m) long.

A female crocodile gently carries her baby from the nest to the river in her mouth.

The female looks after the babies in the shallow water of the river. After about eight weeks the babies go off on their own.

AMAZING REPTILE LIFE CYCLE

Green turtle

The green turtle lives in warm oceans. Green turtles eat underwater plants, such as sea grass. Female green turtles go to the same beach every year to mate and lay eggs.

An adult green turtle can weigh 440 pounds (200 kg).

AMAZING REPTILE FACT

Some females swim about 620 miles (1,000 km) to get to their breeding beach. It can take them weeks!

The adult male and female turtles meet and mate in the shallow water.

Turtles swim by paddling with their flippers.

The females crawl out of the sea and up the beach. The turtle digs a deep hole in the sand with her flippers. She lays her eggs, covers them with sand, and then crawls back to the sea.

The green turtle lays up to 200 eggs.

The baby turtles hatch after about seven weeks. The babies have to look after themselves. They dig themselves out of the sand and dash to the sea.

The tiny turtle hatchlings are in danger of being eaten by predators, such as seabirds.

AMAZING REPTILE LIFE CYCLE

Komodo dragon

The dragon's spit is so full of germs, just one bite can kill its prey.

The Komodo dragon is the world's largest lizard. These giant reptiles live on Komodo Island and four other islands in South East Asia. Komodo dragons hunt for wild pigs and deer. They also eat animals that are already dead.

Male Komodos stand on their back legs to wrestle, to attract a mate.

After mating, the female scrapes out a shallow nest in the ground and lays about 25 eggs. The female then leaves the eggs to hatch on their own.

The dragon's eggs hatch after seven to nine months. The babies climb trees and eat insects and lizards. Trees are safe spaces, because if an adult dragon catches a baby, it will eat it!

This baby dragon is two days old and about 12 inches (30 m) long.

An adult male can be almost 10 feet (3 m) long!

AMAZING REPTILE FACT

A female Komodo dragon in a British zoo laid eggs that hatched into babies even though she had no male around to mate with!

AMAZING AMPHIBIAN LIFE CYCLE

Red-eyed tree frog

Suction pads on their toes to help it stick to leaves.

The red-eyed tree frog lives in rainforests in Central America. Red-eyed tree frogs eat insects.

In the breeding season, male red-eyed tree frogs gather together on branches over a pond.

After mating, the female lays up to 50 eggs on a leaf that's hanging over the pond. Laying lots of eggs in one go means at least some babies will survive.

After about five days the eggs hatch and the tadpoles fall down into the pond below.

When these tadpoles have grown into frogs, they will climb back into the trees.

The males call to females with a clicking noise.

AMAZING AMPHIBIAN FACT

With its eyes closed the frog blends into its green habitat. If attacked, it opens its big red eyes—this startles predators!

A red-eyed tree frog is a nocturnal frog. This means it rests during the day and is active at night.

Surinam Toad

Surinam toads live mainly a solitary life. Their flat body is meant to resemble a leaf floating in the water or a rock. It is perfect for living on muddy river bottoms in South America.

Each finger has a tiny, star-shaped tip, leading to its other name: star-fingered toad.

AMAZING AMPHIBIAN FACT

When the Surinam toad senses movement, it lunges forward and eats its prey— small fish, worms, and crustaceans—in one gulp.

Males call to the females by making a clicking sound underwater. A willing female releases 60 to 100 eggs. The male then fertilizes them and pushes them onto to her back, where they stick to her skin.

During the next few days, her skin grows around the eggs. After hatching, the young toads ride on her back for three to four months, continuing to develop under her skin.

When ready, the young toads pop out of their mother's skin and head for the surface to breath.

AMAZING AMPHIBIAN LIFE CYCLE

Axolotl

The axolotl is an amphibian that looks like a baby even when it is an adult. It is a kind of salamander, but it looks like a giant tadpole. Axolotls live in lakes in Mexico and Central America, but people also keep them as pets.

If an axolotl loses a leg, it can grow another one.

Axolotls mate in water. After mating, the female lays up to 1,000 eggs and sticks them on plants and stones.

AMAZING AMPHIBIAN FACT
Some people in Mexico like to eat axolotls.

The axolotl is about 10 inches (25 cm) long.

The axolotl breathes through gills, not lungs, and never comes out of the water.

The eggs hatch in two to three weeks. The babies eat tiny water animals. Their legs start to grow after about 10 days.

Baby axolotls sometimes eat each other!

That's amazing!

The North American bullfrog lays 25,000 eggs in one go!

Are you ready for some more amazing reptile and amphibian facts? Did you know there's a toad that doesn't have tadpoles, a snake that's as long as six men, and a lizard that's a leftover from prehistoric times?!

The anaconda is the world's heaviest snake. It can weigh up to 550 pounds (250 kg) and grow to 33 feet (10 m) long.

The female anaconda gives birth to up to 80 babies at one time.

Baby tuataras do not hatch from their eggs for 12 to 15 months—the longest time of any reptile.

AMAZING REPTILE FACT

When resting, tuataras may only take one breath an hour!

50% of the body of the wide mouth frog is their mouth. They are known to eat anything and don't know when to stop, including mice and other frogs. They will try to eat something bigger than them even if it means choking to death!

The hairy frog is commonly known as the horror frog. It has an unusual skill. When threatened, it can break its own bones and push them through the skin of their feet to create its own claws.

Glossary

camouflage – colors, marks or a shape that hides an animal from predators, and its prey
deserts – very dry places, that are often sandy or rocky. Deserts can be very hot in the day. Some deserts get cold at night.
ectothermic – an ectothermic animal needs sunshine to warm up and become active
gills – breathing organs (parts of the body) in animals that live in water, like fish and baby amphibians
grasslands – wide open grassy spaces with few trees
hatch – when a baby bird or animal breaks out of its egg
mate – when a male and female animal meet and have babies
predator – an animal which hunts and kills other animals for food
rainforests – forests of tall trees in places with lots of rain
scales – hard plates of skin that cover the bodies of reptiles and fish
stages – different times in an animal's life when the animal changes
temperature – how hot or cold something is
territory – an area or place where an animal feeds and breeds
wetlands – damp places with wet, boggy ground and lots of ponds, lakes or rivers

Index

Picture credits

Shutterstock. 1: Patryk Kosmider. 2-3: jDross75. 4-5: By jeep 2499, By Foto 4440., Karel Gallas, Martin Janca, Elena Erasmus. 6-7: Eric IsShutterstock. 1: Lucy Stacey. 2-3: Shane Myers Photography. 4-5: Kie Studio, Roger de la Harpe. Yasemin G, Starover Sibirak, Rhys Mitchell. 6-7: Tyler McDonald, RMT, Seasonin_17, Scott Hughey. 8-9: Artur Synenko, Ondrej Prosicky, Kamnuan, Marco Maggesi, Dirk Ercken. 10-11: Marco Maggesi, Clear View Stock, Vetlas, Thorsten Spoerlein. 12-13: Achimdiver, Janelle Liugge, Gaschwald, Kurit afshen. 14-15: Reptiles4all, Binu Nair, Deb Davis, Heiko Kiera, Ton Bangkeaw, Hagit Berkovich, Sander Meertins, Eric Lesselee, Linas T, Marius Neascsa. 16-17: Rich Carey, Richard Whitcombe. 18-19: Catchlight Lens. 20-21: Shane Myers Photography, David Evison, IrinaK. 22-23: Luca Vaime, Gudkov Andrey, Rob Haine. 24-25: Worldslifewonders, Gewofreey Newland, Neil Bromhall. 26-27: Rosa Jay, Reptiles4all, Dan Olsen. 28-29: Eric Isselee, Has Asatryan , Kuttelvaserova Stuchelov. 30-31: Christian Ouellet, fRranca, CVraig Walton, Reptiles4all.